SAN

I WONDER IF THERE ARE OTHER PLACES

C T A

AS KNOTTED WITH LIGHT AND SHADE

AHSAHTA PRESS
BOISE, IDAHO

2012

THE NEW SERIES

#44

SANCTA

ANDREW GRACE

Ahsahta Press, Boise State University, Boise, Idaho 83725-1525
http://ahsahtapress.boisestate.edu
http://ahsahtapress.boisestate.edu/books/grace/grace.htm
Cover design by Quemadura
Book design by Janet Holmes
Printed in Canada

LIBRARY OF CONGRESS CATALOGING-IN-PUBLICATION DATA

Grace, Andrew, 1978-
Sancta / Andrew Grace.
p. cm.—(New series ; #44)
ISBN-13: 978-1-934103-24-1 (pbk. : alk. paper)
ISBN-10: 1-934103-24-1 (pbk. : alk. paper)
I. Title.
PS3607.R325S26 2012
811'.6—DC23

2011029410

ACKNOWLEDGMENTS

Sections of this book have been published, sometimes in earlier versions, in *Gulf Stream, LIT, Washington Square, Smartish Pace, Mid-American Review, Seattle Review, Cadillac Cicatrix, 580 Split, H_NGM_N* and *Double Room.*

Thanks to my family for their unending support. Thanks also to Stanford University's creative writing program for providing me with a Stegner Fellowship during which this book was written.

These poems borrow phrases from William Carlos Williams, Ralph Waldo Emerson, Guy Davenport, Henry David Thoreau, Edward Arlington Robinson, James Merrill and Nick Cave.

FOR TORY

Grief is the never ender in the raucous pond reeds. Ursa Minor sets out its silver lice in the cypress. Take one season and turn through it like these fruit bats, following sent-back abyss-ticks, *here*, and further out, *here* . . . I wanted this to be an epigraph. I wanted to rain for forty days. I wanted a trigger. I have a lake with a crown of bats. I have intransience. Salt away.

The cabin, once my father's, is a tenth of a mile from the lake. Between, wetlands where loose-rooted trees jut at wrong angles, propped by the anchored pines. Pitcher plants unfurl their crystal abattoirs. The bulrushes' heads disintegrate into a carpet. After crossing over waterlogged planks, you come to a short rocky beach, then the ashen lake. In short, this place is a sanctum of all there is to lose.

The lake's nerves burn with light. You are a sepia notch among the moonlit reeds. I am at the lake's shore. The wind is tearing at asp, water, us. This is Chapter 1, in which we try to profit by forgetting we eternally are you and I. We are foreign in the rich oil of the dark. We collect in dark sockets. We are the form of a form dismantled.

In other words, we are broken mirrors. Your skin is silver lamina of lakewater. My hair is an asterisk of sticks. Your tongue is larval. There are objects along the shore so undone we can only call them remnants. Deathless matter. There is joy in this, the resilience of what's left. The hypodermic needle's glint, archipelago of Coke. The bones that will crowd out the lake. Flesh devout as junk.

What does a white sky *not* resemble? Salt fathoms. Vodka. What I imagine the mind to look like: expectant screen onto which synapses erupt like sparrows. Frontmatter. Pale vacuo. Shower curtain behind which some man fills his arms with himself. Tell me what you see in me. A voice that alone could roil water, but then—? A voice alone? I never knew whose cipher I was until everyone stopped listening.

Across the lake there is an old cement factory; behind it a mall only visible from here by the light from the parking lot lamps. The mall is one condition of exile: we can quarantine ourselves from our own history, but not from the greenish blaze of a building the elderly circle like a seven story mountain, while inside the young try on skins like they are new to death.

At first, the sky is all cinders and oil. The ribs of heaven clutch its disc of sulfur. Then constellations are snuffed like dream-sites in the stirring mind. As if we are to choose, the beach lays out its castoffs: wrench, rain-soaked checkbook, paper napkin. The light swivels and shows us an ache that is not bleak. There is so much light we can't keep it out of our eyes.

Exit cabin. You walk the woods as if in a hospital ward: noiselessly, with some sense of guilt about being whole. Silhouettes rave in the backlight. I ask you a question and you let it blear across the silence. Exit sun. Your snared attention flails in your gray eyes. When we reach the lake, there are elderly couples walking like incurables taking the air. We walk in step with them.

My father took off his glasses with the same slowness he used to clean blood off his knife. He proceeded to tell me stories about whaling fleets. I thought of the whale's voice, its sick-on-a-journey blues. Its death like a burning ship. And father's moral: essentially the ship *was* on fire when the cook's boy fell asleep on duty. My father always smiled like a knife was between his teeth.

I read: the following are detriments to memory: gazing on moveable things suspended in air, the reading of periodicals, frequent laughter, eating of unripe fruit, reading tombstones in graveyards. I could add jogging miles beyond your body's limit, stoking a sodium-flare of longing in your chest. My legs hum in their wrack as I literally think of nothing, its seasons and sky, its sheer exhaustion we can only call wholesome.

Golf balls glow under a thin membrane of water. The car-gored buck by the roadside has yet to break out in insects. All is still. This is the Chapter in which nothing happens. I would cancel my blood if I could, to make it more silent. We are in bed. On days like this, our faces are oceans receding. We are nothing's crest. I almost draw you closer to me.

Let's play storm metaphor. The lake gone grand mal with lightning, florid scrape, sick hands, sulfuric hair of wrecked sisters. Now your turn. Light akin to breaking skin. A shower of **X**s. A sword down the mouth of the sky. You win again. This is the Chapter in which I can't stop shivering. Your face is lit by pure exhaustion. The light rends. God help the whites of our eyes.

I dream another me exists in a cabin by a lake, reading aloud from what I have written. Carnage in the North Territories. The medicinal properties of light. The etymology of the word *lake*, which I conjecture to be a combination of *lack* and *wake*. I have written so much. The pages fill the room. For every blank page, I'll breathe one less breath. For every filled page, two less.

I record the bray of the black squirrel in my notebook. I record the flakes of sparrows, the ash scrum of the lake, a sky the color of heroin, the stutter of a distant mall, how some trees wear their own blood, smoke verbatim from smoke I once saw when an entire landscape burned. Some days I want to walk until I die of exposure or the lack of it.

Leafless trees hold up their cricket legs to the sky. Sound-less. Your fragmented jigsaw aches with symbolism as you arch over it. Your hair, the color of a violin, hangs unwashed around your face. Unstrung morning, whose elements add up blissfully to zero. The puzzle approaches its image, but a ragged absence of center holds you in limbo. My love, today we could live on nothing but revision and silence.

Hush in, mist in, we walk the lake's littered shore. I crack a deer's bone over someone's dock. A single fish is caught in a tide pool eight feet from the lake proper. There is hardly enough water to swim in. I think of the difficulty with which the dead must move. Do they see us? It must be like trying to open your eyes when they are already open.

I read: *not to copy nature, NOT, prostrate to copy nature*
. . . An aborted storm makes the horizon crooked. But the
man said not to copy nature. Imitate it. A field of women
makes my memory crooked. My mind invents wind to
scatter them, but they do not scatter. They are waiting
for me to wreck my life. I have, and I have. The women
still wait with the fortitude of storm.

The brambles rule. They have claimed the west lakefront.
A chorus of snared plastic bags hisses with the wind. The
thorns clutch Nehi cans, newspapers whose emergencies
the light has stolen, semblances of nests looted of their
young, rags of post-prom degeneration and other acts of
barbs' thievery. The shoe orphans are going nowhere.
And neither am I, locked into what catches and doesn't,
and which is among the destitute.

How many birds have you killed, and how much space would their spent bodies take up? A bucket? An attic? When I would drink, I wished my fists full of sparrows. To eliminate transcendence, even physical, was the goal. To raze an apex. In the blotting out of memory, I wanted to be in the skeleton crew, to labor the night long until the sparrows resumed their bright, ruined Assisi.

From 3 in the Morning Part 1: The fish jerk shad-flies
from the lake's surface. I sit by a fire and eat fish that
tastes like a brown paper bag salted. You are on the end of
someone's dock in the wind. Your hair is like a shredded
flag. One night—remember?—you traded places with
your sadness. You were absolute. You shook, exhilarated.
You haven't asked for permission since.

From 3 in the Morning Part 2: When you don't want to be consoled, the shell of a country music song drifts across the lake. When I confess to you, a woman in white appears at an open window. When the clouds come to a dead stop, I am quickened into clay. When the iron shadows hunker down, you unload the little boat of your sorrow and we climb aboard.

From 3 in the Morning Part 3: The cabin irks and repents us. We drink the dust of trying to solve each other. Maybe it was you and that boy in a room of charred paint. Maybe it was my silence. You call your childhood *My Mother Says Don't Stare*. I call mine *A Screen Door Slams Shut*. We give up, find that a scream is better than a thesis.

You tell me we need to talk as if we are surrounded by people instead of trees. You talk about fields of quiet that bloom in your sleep, how the dead elm mannequins seem to move closer each day, how, if candles can stare, they stare. You say this place feels *posthumous*. I had to face away to say that's what I like about it. Expecting that, you'd already gone.

What woke me. You are asleep. The cabin is quiet. Out
on the deck, ants form a script that spells nothing. Noth-
ing hangs like a colony of bats under the asp. The sun
nourishes its shadows. I woke to the sound of a bruise
spreading. Bourbon hums in the cabinet. Where shall I
wander. As to a new country where I wake to darkness
and displace nothing as I rise.

You want to walk to the villas a mile up the beach. The reedy voices of children reach us here at the cabin and sift down my neck like loose hair. But you are drawn to them, and want to see the playground, always empty at the hour we pass by it, full of life. The dusk's light collects its wage of ashes. I agree, just as the voices fade.

File under: I don't know if this ever happened but I feel I need to distract you from oncoming low-level panic attack. Once, as a light crept across the gnash of narrow ice, gripping small trees, bat harmonics shrill in the spruce-scent, eyes closed, I groped for miles along the low purr of powerlines. The blindness grew familiar. Slowly, inside my mouth, a mouth of silver teeth began to open.

Each hour is a puzzle that must be solved to pass. The first hour is a hole to be dug to find a chest, and inside that chest is the second hour and a shovel. The fifth hour is a mockingbird raving in code. The ninth hour is a crate of smoke and only surrender can save us. The labyrinth of the eleventh hour turns frail when we charge through.

My own unsoundness has a strange history. It started at school when I was young. A man said, "Heartily know, / When half-gods go / The gods arrive." Which was I? If choosing, I would've been the second: effortless, regally sad, clothed in ancient light. But I knew better. I felt as transgressable as anything. And I still do like dark little sayings that cleave like salt to the tongue.

I have lost the plot of the story you are telling; the flat clear nouns you release into the air dissipate like fleet herds between us. You say something about using the sleight-of-eye an onion makes for sadness to your advantage. Then a sudden storm, gone too quickly to believe in. Rain-cooled brimstone seeps up as today's dusk. Like me, the last light feints focus. Thus we are all liars.

I am careful not to justify myself. I am vacant as rain. I discover an ancient wreck under the porch and cover it with leaves. I occupy an outpost, call myself a samurai, don't speak for three days and become so full of death I can't taste anything. Then I speak. A proverb tastes like metallic water. A confession tastes like burnt sage. Prayer is like syrup: ipecac or simple.

In some other life, I was leaning on a railing. Your face
appeared. The silence took a quarter-turn towards me. I
made an indefinite gesture. You approached nonetheless.
O the white rock of your face, a cold hill with clear shad-
ows running across it. Or so it seemed in that city where,
in the lamp-studded dark, the black eyes of traffic looked
only at you: penumbra's blind spot, bright form.

I keep expecting a small, feral animal to be in the cabin with me. To stare at me with the soft, terrible eyes in which there is always snow. To be as still as I am. In this cabin it is always September. A penultimate fall, only aware of itself by what it spills. (Flour and hair.) Only articulated in burnt grammar. (Sorry and ash.) I keep expecting to be.

The bridge is made of names. *Steve + Nancy 4Ever, Suicidal Tendencies* (crossed out), *Fuck Gina*. Beneath, the lake's bottleneck has become a place for flyfishermen to cast line so thin from here it is invisible, making of their act a pantomime of men working kinks out of the air. ~~This bridge allows me to jump off and yet remain still~~. Or ~~it would, if I could just remain still~~.

I read: *Love is the long sword; desire is the sword; lust is the short sword; sex is the dagger*—Ryoto, who died of hara-kiri, slicing a cross into his stomach. I used to cut my left arm before I knew you. "To focus," but really to flaunt pain, like a carnival barker *Come one   Come all   If I could stir   I could break a tree   I could break you.*

This is the Chapter in which everything changes. You are gone. A cab's double script unspools down the dirt. I remember driving you somewhere. Snow purged an obscure thirst of a parched, white sky. We talked about the life after our deaths. Unwashed in an abandoned land. Houses on fire, or else, the escort of fire. A march forthcoming. We walk would upright, salt wandering to salt. Late and far.

At the mercy of a broken sleep. Computer screen in a dark room. The cabin is barely scotched to the night's side. Now I even miss how you retreated from me. The living room is a deep well. This is not a nocturne. This is not even a mood. This is black water at the back of the mind, rocking. This is a letter from the torn country of fact.

I think my mind is touched. Filleted by the wakeful. The grey lake beats its two hearts together. I sprang to the stirrup and fell among the nettles because there was never a horse and I anon am lesioned by B L A. I turn on the stereo until Kurt Cobain's koans turn platitudes. In a dreamt Civil War I worked in a makeshift hospital. Men shuddered and sank. I "helped" them.

If I can rise from the dust, I cannot answer. If I can move, a single body, as if I were in a large group, and I the tour guide to this old bog washed by the rag of fall light, and someone who is not there asked me a question about where the others in the group had gone, I cannot answer. If I can answer, I cannot sleep.

I have been letting the cold in at night. No fire, door cracked. The cold is so thick it is like a threat, a blade against the neck. So thick you could tear off pieces of it and put them under your tongue. Colder than a stone lion, a talon or a star. I hold my skin up to it. Cold teaches this: you are not yet tired. Or strong.

Every morning the rip widens. I strip the bed and lay on the slick stitched diamonds on the mattress. I imagine an angel on my right shoulder that whispers *be practical*. The devil on the left walks the synthetic terrain like it is walking something on a leash, but nothing leads his extended right hand. Maybe he is the one unraveling the sheets? No, he is tracing where I slept.

Moth morning, maelstrom of mothwing at the window, fog-dulled sun trundled like a cart of moths across the aspirin sky. I stay in bed. Deer dance the bolero across the path. I used to count moths to sleep, each chewed-through cocoon an act not of transformation, but of violence against the past. The history of a moth is my history. Mesh-like, the world held me. I escaped. Or it did.

Disconcert of thrush and thrush. Beachfire grapples with itself as if trying to not be made-of-my-hands. But I have never been more myself. The forest knocks and I answer. I am the dropped stitch that keeps the history of this place from being complete. The lake is a necklace of light and I am its negative pendant, brilliance's absence. Maybe I overstate things. Maybe I am my own thrown voice.

The sounds of garbage trucks climax in the villas. Terns prick the sky. This is the first Chapter with snow inside of it. The cabin clinches its December coma and I wonder at my staying here. The feedback of the truck's incisors is like the whinny of a horse carrying off one of the Damned after his last request, to, in some lake, swim the liquor out of his skin.

Snow. The comfort of its arc. It makes me feel clean, like I can ferret out of their holes the darkest thoughts in my mind and sun them a little. I walk to the lake. It swallows the whole white confused mass. It's subject to nothing. To not be the man I woke up as, to not kick the straw dog or lavish loss on the tangible, seems almost here.

The light on the lake gains focus, as if God had just risen
from sleep and said to himself "Let's see what's Mine."
Well, for one, that swimmer lost in magnesium. That cache
of rain-soaked fireworks some blackened fingers forgot.
The antics of the light, again diffused. What's mine? This
left foot that turns home, the grandeur of sadness on a
Sunday. As in, my leviathan silence. My blank flag.

The cold gives me my father's hunger. I cannot live on nuts, herb-tea and elegies. I am full of blood. I tune my brain to a burnt frequency and do push-ups until I feel like I am underwater. Blessed was the day my father in hipboots woke me early and made me shovel with him. I was wild with tearing at a real core. He had to make me stop.

Today a horse swam in the lake. A man waited for it on the shore. Its frenzied gait hidden under brown water, only its head is visible, as if unfastened from its labor. It looks terrified. Yet it goes further, almost beyond the tree-line's reflection. It sinks lower. It is not terrified, but elated. This is bliss. The hot thrum of your body grappling with what it cannot depend on.

I read: "Nature has no nothing." What about a lone hunk of cement in a stand of pines? Emblem of a house unbuilt, but there was never a house here. This close to the lake the soil is too wet to set a foundation on. It is free of referents. It will keep me honest by its singularity, when I talk with others. Or, better, I will forget it entirely.

The wind scrolls through its clichés: cracked whip, exhalation, the dead's turnstile, aftermath of a moth's flight, wake of something too big to see . . . A blade of ducks skins the blankness. All ants wear elegies on their backs. Hatchlings find their pond to drown in. The world is so casual: it presumes its attrition. I envy a self-cleaning apparatus. And the wind pushes another load of used light over the horizon.

I am conversant in things ex. The era of wild apples is over; snow has taken all the November out of the sky. I feel like charging at the world like an amnesiac hungry for the smell of charcoal, a starling's upswing, the name in the mirror. The unknown is a bride that has been walking away from me for centuries. Give me a fresh elsewhere to drench in self.

A convergence of kayaks makes the lake cross-eyed. They greet each other as if they meant to meet here, then pass each other after elegant gestures. If I choose to be alone, to nurse a black canyon behind my teeth, to rehearse the afterlife and, at every turn in the endless path, startle three wolves opening up a deer, what of it? Doesn't *choosing* this make it sane? *Answer me.*

Sortes biblicae: telling one's fortune by opening the Bible at random. "Do not let the sun go down while you are still angry, and do not give the devil a foothold." Better hurry. I chop wood like I am smashing a Stratocaster, all splinters and misses. Wasps storm the bruised peaches. An owl sits like a jar of blood overhead. Lord, I axed a milksnake and took pills to sleep.

The lake is like a parchment rent open by use and time. Whatever was written on it cannot be blinked back to perfection. I wish I could tell you in other than words how the light goes gray, lemon, glue, then gash. How up close this tuft of pine looks like the blueprint of a bridge. Am I a citizen of these images? Or an interloper? Or just a voice?

The phone rang: it was you. As always, no sleep is Pyr-
rhic. The sun is now up and the edges of trees have firmed
up in the subzero light. Last night, the rasped bass note
of the past rode the hours down to no crescendo. The
struck flint of my tongue gave no flame. I walk into the
chill luminance to speak to what cannot speak back, but
still does.

I stoke the stove livid. I want to treat dry heat like a mirror: in that low belly of blue efficiency, form is undone more honestly than ever. Better than earth, which feigns to embrace what enters it. Better than the willful tantrums of air. Better even than water, which removes but preserves forms in the museum of no eye. Let my attention feed like fire, from the inside out.

Remembering when you were here is like nailing horse-shoes to hoof-prints; trying too late to protect days that were unshod and now dissolve at the speed of breath. Spiders turn back to repairing the crippled sky. Eaves weep new icicles after a freak heat stole the old. The clock's patience grows wild. Almost absently, I stir my pain so as to keep my reflection from assembling in its dark water.

The icicles' chipped teeth are shot through with Novo-
cain of sunlight. When I practice begging you to return,
I am reminded that the tongue is a muscle that needs con-
ditioning. Say *Goodbye* or *Please* 1,000 times to yourself
so that you never have to say them out loud. Stand in the
cold until your mouth is numb and pray in slow motion
to the distant gods of the present winter.

The distant ricks sizzle in an ecclesiastical light. The orchard's corridors have never been less haunted. *God knows his own* rings over the landscape like a tuning fork, cleaning everything with the chlorine of divine attention. At least that's how it feels to me, unshaven, homesick for literally God knows what. May it be my father burning leaves. May it be in the blessed house of all I don't remember.

The moon snitches on a clutch of skunks. Another rack
of cloud scrolls over. At times, the eye seems charnel
house of the known and can only be slaked by novelty:
that lavish other. It wants to turn down a corner of para-
dise. But tonight the eye seems instrument only, stunned
as a lighthouse's strobe. The marred moon hectors itself
clear as if witness is all I am good for.

Out walking, stirred a sorority of sparrows. I am not sick or well; I am luke-sick and free. This is the Chapter where wood and water stand quite still and I make nothing of it. I could say, *Do penance and disappear.* Or *When I die you will find swamp oak written on my heart*. But I'll not even kneel. My mouth is seamed as a scar, debarred and redeemed.

There are shoeprints in front of the cabin—some hunter bent on silence in the glassy fields, some stranger who could eye me from afar and see me as his own ghost, take my hesitations along the slick path as his regrets, my switchbacks as repentance, my leaving as his choice to return to the lush sleeve of his body. Blessed are the risen. May the risen-from also be blessed.

I respect most the saints who've refused me. St. Christopher. St. Thesalie of the seventh heaven. St. Lennox of the hundred hands, so generous it is not to be beloved. St. Philip of one element studied endlessly, of the local knowledge that illuminates other quarters. Most of all, St. Dante of the born across, light among the hot ruck of shadows—today let my self burn hard in its absence.

If only it was a sin to drink the lake water; to step down into that opaque stuff, shot through with clay churned by your entering, the wake of silt unfurling behind you like a dun gown as you walk deeper, the train of your vague regalia licks the surface and settles, leaving you anonymous, bent at the waist to cup the water to your mouth: not given, stolen.

Bulrushes gone to seed loll like the heads of the dead. "I am as one who never shuts his eyes," says one. Another, "No matter what I think, I think of it." "It's not the darkness we die of," says a little more mind spilt into thin wind. Or so it seemed, on my way to the lake to watch the sky once again lose itself in its black habit.

Rabbits scratch hours open. The bat wheels like a dirty
medallion around the neck of a beech. Moles, nature's
monks, make tillage their tithe. I am the only breathing
one that's motionless, playing back the before and after
of a loss or two. An orphaned raccoon lopes under the
deck, triple-checking the crusts it has banked for the
cold night. Like me, it has found a way to live during.

Better than reading a tree's rings to learn its history is to see its torn roots after it has fallen in wetlands, its pale foundation laid bare by untenable mud. A Medusa's head: blind roots caught mid-grope, as if trying to nurse the dry air. It is a wreath of struggle. Now lichen and bracket mushrooms set up their frail kingdom. I almost believe God cannot be unkind to us.

I always had to calculate the square root of my father's speech. He would answer questions I didn't ask. As in, when we were in the fishing boat and, after clubbing the radiant muscle of a trout to death, he said, "I *can* be proud of you." Or, on the way home, floodlighting the moccasin-sliced mist, when he said, "*Huge animals leap away into darkness.* Now you tell the story."

Bernie at Ward Brothers advertises they are still doing well on steelheads, fishing 30 feet of water with crawler harnesses. The salmon season is over, but fishing for the big kings is still quite good. The mollusk census is at capacity until the thrashers peck open their brittle mantles. Chokecherries blaze the path closed. I hunt what insect voided the dahlias. Crows rake open dust. Small war to small war.

Woke to creaky sunlight. Turned up the fire's dry volume and watched a black squirrel wolf down a pile of seed. Later, a shower of hard granules of snow fell and I stood on the porch listening to the huge hiss in the trees. I used to believe I was very good at being lonely. Now it doesn't seem to matter, as the snowfall softens and doesn't make a sound.

The abandon of the pileated can be frightening. Its gun-hammer neck makes to crack its beak into shards, just to suss out one puce beetle hidden in a wrinkle of bark. It is willing to break itself for hunger. This is the rigor that life takes, I tell myself. I wade into the frigid lake and repeat *Pain is weakness leaving the body* and hope to God it isn't true.

I read: "To some will come a time when change itself is beauty, if not heaven." Not me. You only change twice. Death is one. The other is when you are in the woods and time tumbles like a burnt leaf under a chemical bath sky, and you walk to the lake, plunge, and rise changed. Nothing to do with redemption, but with the knowledge that death is still one.

If a man alone in a cabin falls to his knees, does anyone hear him? Before sunrise he easily mistakes frost for blossoms, the stunned tableau framed into triptych by the cabin's sliding doors. If a cardinal, descending, becomes the scene's only movement and he reads it as a metaphor for his pain's trajectory descending from mind to a throat closed around prayer, can we hear how his silence alters?

I read: "Have I become my senses, all else gone?" That's how it feels this morning in the woods, my pulse like a rag on a nail in an intermittent wind, air the fragrance of smoke and someone's hair, the dog-crushed ice at lake's edge unspooling like a baroque motif down the beach, where my vision fails and abstractions melt into the un-differentiated blue I've always wanted to call home.

One regret settles like a moth on my knuckle. I am in
a room whose wallpaper is thin rain. This is a dream
or what is found in the mind's channel zero. The moth
scans its head back and forth mechanically. It seems to be
searching for the next place to land. Be quiet. The future
is making a decision. It lifts, nestles in my ear. It says
forgive me.

Don't you get sick of decadence? Even if these woods were bare, they would be overwhelmingly pure. Their white would be wolf-white and would not dissolve when you shut your eyes. Do you ever feel like description is a filibuster against emotion? Today is boredom and the scent of cedar. I used to chide myself for being satisfied. Now I watch the lake's mirror etc. and I sing etc., etc.

Look, is all. The cabin. Look. The lake. Flies like quarter-carats of Hell festoon the curtain. Slipped fires take to the sky. Sweet pine strewn with nude opal birds at its base. O if only my attention led to something besides more attention. A reward beyond what's there: cloud, stone, rust, black seeds, silence. At least the darkening wood seems to answer me. *All right. But quietly. Into your coat.*

I wonder if there are other places as knotted with light and shade, as scarfed with burnt mist as this acre. I wonder if the next lake's man is home free. I wonder if I ever believed the darkening wood answered me. It didn't. I am starting to believe in the next lake, the other acre. Come sanctum. Come along strict witness. Look. The eye of a leaf is all.

All is raw edges. The cement plant's single claw of smoke arcs over the lake. Puddles are blitzed by the blood fly hatch. Without sleep, my eyes have gnats in front of them where there are none. I stayed up watching the only badger I have ever seen ransack my trashcan. I win victories over the ordinary eye. I've learned: this light will never end if I don't let it.

This morning is choked with stones. A dead boat battery acts nonchalant in the reeds. The shore's recesses are full of black tadpoles. Shape-shifters. They drift slowly in unison across the puddle, like negative snow. I should be thinking about myself, about how I should change. Such a mirror. But I don't—I *should* change, find the form I could burn in. But these unworkable days are mine and empty.

Tonight I will leave the cabin. The stars begin to gnarl in the corners of the sky. I've had enough of nursing my senses awake: they are keened to any vestige of God. When I say God I mean any way of navigating the radiant aftermath of loss. And what I mean by radiance is what the lake is doing, marbled by the moonlight and shaking like a lost man.

ANDREW GRACE lives in Cincinnati with his wife Tory and daughter Lily. His other books include *A Belonging Field* (Salt) and *Shadeland* (Ohio State University Press).

AHSAHTA PRESS

SAWTOOTH POETRY PRIZE SERIES

2002: Aaron McCollough, *Welkin* (Brenda Hillman, judge)

2003: Graham Foust, *Leave the Room to Itself* (Joe Wenderoth, judge)

2004: Noah Eli Gordon, *The Area of Sound Called the Subtone* (Claudia Rankine, judge)

2005: Karla Kelsey, *Knowledge, Forms, The Aviary* (Carolyn Forché, judge)

2006: Paige Ackerson-Kiely, *In No One's Land* (D. A. Powell, judge)

2007: Rusty Morrison, *the true keeps calm biding its story* (Peter Gizzi, judge)

2008: Barbara Maloutas, *the whole Marie* (C. D. Wright, judge)

2009: Julie Carr, *100 Notes on Violence* (Rae Armantrout, judge)

2010: James Meetze, *Dayglo* (Terrance Hayes, judge)

2011: Karen Rigby, *Chinoiserie* (Paul Hoover, judge)

AHSAHTA PRESS

NEW SERIES

This book is set in Apollo MT type
with Engravers MT titles
by Ahsahta Press at Boise State University
Cover design by Quemadura.
Book design by Janet Holmes.

AHSAHTA PRESS

2012

JANET HOLMES, DIRECTOR
JODI CHILSON, MANAGING EDITOR

KYLE CRAWFORD

CHARLES GABEL

KATE HOLLAND

WALLY HUMPHRIES

TORIN JENSEN

JESSICA JOHNSON, *intern*

GENNA KOHLHARDT

JULIE STRAND

JASON STEPHENS, *intern*

MATT TRUSLOW

ZACH VESPER